The Filippo Berio Me

We've created this meal plan with a week's worth of delicious vegan recipes, which you can mix and match or meal prep to suit you! You can find the full recipes on our website.

	BREAKFAST	LUNCH	DINNER	SNACKS
MONDAY	Superfood Energy Bars	Sicilian Cous Cous Salad	Asparagus and Pea Spaghetti	Sweet Potato Hummus with Vegetables
TUESDAY	Cranberry and Pear Porridge	Roasted Cauliflower and Chickpea Bowls	Broccoli Pesto with Penne	Green Olive Oil Smoothie
WEDNESDAY	Brett Cobley's Chocnut Granola	Stuffed Butternut Squash	Spring Vegetable Pistou	Garlic Flat Breads and Dips
THURSDAY	Simple Avocado on Toast	Peach and Tenderstem Broccoli Salad	Spelt Risotto with Butternut Squash	Courgette and Mint Fritters with Aioli
FRIDAY	Orange Olive Oil Smoothie	Cauliflower, Fig and Hazelnut Farro Salad	Aranchini (using left over risotto) and vegetables of choice	Fruit Kebabs with Chocolate Sauce
SATURDAY	Brett Cobley's Fiery Potato Cakes	Tuscan Bean Stew	Sweet Potato Gnocchi with Walnut Pesto	Cappuccino Olive Oil Cake
SUNDAY	Banana and Oat Muffins	Caramelised Onion and Mushroom Pissaladiere	Spicy Sausages with Cavolo Nero	Stracciatella Olive Oil Ice Cream

Garlic Flat Breads and Dips

These garlic flat breads are so simple to make, requiring only six ingredients and no baking! Serve them with one or more of the three tasty dip options. Each one is packed full of flavour and guaranteed to impress at dinner parties.

Garlic Flat Bread

Serves 6-8
Prep 30 mins
Cook 10 mins

350 g	plain flour, plus extra for dusting
1 tsp	baking powder
½ tsp	salt
350 g	soya yogurt
4 tbsp	Filippo Berio Extra Virgin Olive Oil
2	garlic cloves, crushed

1 Mix together the Filippo Berio Extra Virgin Olive Oil and garlic in a bowl and leave to one side for the oil to infuse.

2 Place the flour, baking powder and salt in a large bowl. Using a spoon, stir in the soya yogurt and mix the ingredients together until roughly combined. Using clean hands, bring everything together.

3 Lightly dust the worktop with a little flour, then knead the mixture together for about 2 minutes to make a smooth dough.

4 Cut the dough in half, then cut each half into 6 pieces. Shape into 12 ovals, then roll out onto a lightly floured surface until they are about 2mm thick.

5 Place a large griddle pan over a high heat. When hot, add the flat breads and cook for 1-2 minutes each side until puffed up and marked with the griddle lines, turning with tongs.

6 Brush the warm breads with the garlic oil and serve immediately with the dips.

Pea & White Bean Hummus

200 g	frozen peas
200 g	tinned cannellini beans, drained and rinsed
1	garlic clove, crushed
1 tbsp	tahini
2 tbsp	lemon juice
2 tbsp	Filippo Berio Extra Virgin Olive Oil
	salt and freshly ground black pepper

Cook the peas in a pan of boiling water, for 2 minutes until just tender. Drain and refresh under cold water. Drain well.

Place the peas, beans, garlic, tahini, lemon juice, Filippo Berio Extra Virgin Olive Oil, in a food processor and blend until smooth. Season to taste.

Artichoke & Mint Dip

400 g	tinned artichoke hearts, drained
50 g	toasted pine nuts
	finely grated zest and juice of 1 small lemon
2 tbsp	Filippo Berio Extra Virgin Olive Oil
	handful of mint leaves
	salt and freshly ground black pepper
	smoked paprika, for sprinkling

Place the artichokes, most of the pine nuts, lemon zest and juice, Filippo Berio Extra Virgin Olive Oil, mint leaves and seasoning in a food processor and blitz until smooth. Spoon into a bowl, sprinkle with the remaining pine nuts and a little smoked paprika, and drizzle with Filippo Berio Extra Virgin Olive Oil.

Cashew & Kale Dip

150 g	cashews, soaked in warm water for 1 hour and drained
50 g	shredded kale leaves
1	garlic clove, crushed
75 ml	Filippo Berio Extra Virgin Olive Oil
2 tbsp	lemon juice
2 tbsp	cold water
	salt and freshly ground black pepper

Place the kale in a bowl and pour over boiling water to cover. Leave to stand for 2 minutes. Drain well and squeeze out excess water. Place in a food processor with the cashews and garlic and process until finely chopped. Add the Filippo Berio Extra Virgin Olive Oil, lemon juice, water and season well. Blend until smooth and adjust seasoning to taste.

Spring Vegetable Pistou Soup

Serves 4
Prep 15 mins
Cook 25 mins

2 tbsp	Filippo Berio Classico Olive Oil
1	onion, chopped
1	garlic clove, crushed
600 ml	vegetable stock
300 g	baby new potatoes, halved or quartered
350 g	baby carrots, quartered
200 g	baby courgettes, quartered
4	tomatoes, chopped
150 g	fresh garden peas
150 g	broad beans, skins removed

This flavoursome soup is a festival of vibrant spring vegetables, made even more delicious with a dollop of garlicky, herby pistou. Pistou is similar to traditional Ligurian pesto, however there is no pine nuts and it's originally made without cheese. There is an option to add vegan Mediterranean style cheese in this pistou.

For the pistou

4	garlic cloves
30	fresh basil leaves
120 ml	Filippo Berio Extra Virgin Olive Oil
50 g	finely grated vegan Mediterranean style cheese, optional

1 Heat the Filippo Berio Classico Olive Oil in a large saucepan and cook the onion and garlic for 2-3 minutes, until softened. Pour over the stock, bring to the boil and add the potatoes. Cover and simmer for 10 minutes.

2 Stir in the carrots, courgette and tomatoes, cover and simmer for 5 minutes. Add the peas and broad beans and cook for 4-5 minutes, until tender. Season to taste.

3 Meanwhile make the pistou: place the garlic and basil in a food processor and blend to a paste, gradually add the Filippo Berio Extra Virgin Olive Oil. Season to taste and stir in the vegan cheese, if using.

4 Ladle the soup into bowls and serve each with a spoonful of the pistou and crusty bread.

Tuscan Bean Stew

Serves 4
Prep 10 mins
Cook 30 mins

3 tbsp	Filippo Berio Classico Olive Oil
1	garlic clove, crushed
2	leeks, sliced
200 g	celeriac, peeled and cut into 1.5 cm pieces
2	carrots, sliced
2	sprigs fresh rosemary
75 g	pearl barley, rinsed
400 g	tinned chopped tomatoes
2 tbsp	sun-dried tomato purée
600 ml	vegetable stock
	salt and freshly ground black pepper
400 g	tinned borlotti beans, drained and rinsed
200 g	cavolo nero or curly kale, tough stems removed and roughly chopped
	Filippo Berio Extra Virgin Olive Oil, for drizzling
	crusty bread, for serving

Like most Italian cuisine, Tuscan cooking relies on fresh and simple local ingredients to make hearty meals packed full of flavour. This stew is no exception with a delicious mixture of vegetables, beans and barley. The perfect warming and nutritious meal for colder Autumn evenings.

1 Heat the Filippo Berio Classico Olive Oil in a large saucepan, add the garlic, leeks, celeriac, carrots and sprigs of rosemary and cook for 3-4 minutes. Stir in the pearl barley.

2 Add the tomatoes, sun-dried tomato purée, stock and season well. Bring to the boil, reduce the heat, cover and simmer for 25 minutes, or until the pearl barley and vegetables are just tender.

3 Stir in the beans and cavolo nero, cover and cook for a further 5 minutes. Serve the stew in bowls, with a drizzle of Filippo Berio Extra Virgin Olive Oil, with crusty bread to mop up the juices.

Roasted Cauliflower and Chickpea Bowls

Cauliflower is a versatile and inexpensive vegetable that has long been used in Italian cuisine. For this recipe we've roasted cauliflower in Middle Eastern herbs and spices, which transforms it from a humble vegetable into a delicious centre piece.

Serves 4
Prep 15 mins
Cook 30 mins

1	whole cauliflower, cut into small florets
2 tbsp	Filippo Berio Mild & Light Olive Oil
2 tsp	sumac
2 tsp	za'atar
	salt and freshly ground black pepper
1	lemon, halved
400 g	tinned chickpeas, drained and rinsed
1 tbsp	tahini
2 tbsp	Filippo Berio Extra Virgin Olive Oil
75 g	baby spinach leaves
2	carrots, peeled and coarsely grated
250 g	pouch cooked quinoa
	handful pomegranate seeds

1 Preheat the oven to 200°C, Gas Mark 6.

2 Place the cauliflower florets in a large bowl and add the Filippo Berio Mild & Light Olive Oil, the sumac, za'atar and season. Turn to coat in the oil and spices, then place in a roasting tin with the lemon halves and roast for 20 minutes.

3 Remove the lemon, turn over the cauliflower florets, stir in the chickpeas and cook for 10 minutes.

4 Squeeze the juice from the warm lemons into a bowl, whisk with the tahini and Filippo Berio Extra Virgin Olive Oil. Season to taste.

5 Divide the quinoa between 4 bowls and add the cauliflower and chickpeas, the spinach leaves and carrots.

6 Drizzle over the dressing and scatter with the pomegranate seeds. Serve immediately.

Cook's tip: *Don't throw away the liquid from your tinned chickpeas – it's a useful ingredient and can be stored in the fridge for up to a week.*

Courgette and Mint Fritters with Aioli

Courgette is another versatile vegetable with a delicate flavour. Here, we use them to make these light fritters paired with a delicious Mediterranean inspired aioli sauce.

Serves 4
Prep 20 mins
Cook 15 mins

For the aioli

3 tbsp	chickpea water, from a can
1 tbsp	Filippo Berio White Wine Vinegar
½ tsp	salt
125 ml	Filippo Berio Mild & Light Olive Oil
1	fat garlic clove, crushed
1 tsp	lemon juice

For the fritters

2	large courgettes, coarsely grated
150 g	cooked grains, such as freekeh or bulgar wheat
4	spring onions, chopped
4 tbsp	freshly chopped mint
1	small red chilli, deseeded and chopped
125 g	self-raising flour
1 tsp	baking powder
1 tbsp	Filippo Berio Mild & Light Olive Oil plus extra for frying
300 ml	vegan milk
	salt and freshly ground black pepper

1 For the aioli, place the chickpea water, Filippo Berio White Wine Vinegar and salt in a food processor and blend until combined. Slowly add the Filippo Berio Mild & Light Olive Oil with the motor running, making sure it is fully combined before adding more. Add the lemon juice and garlic and mix. Place in the fridge.

2 Place the courgettes in a tea towel and squeeze out the excess water. Place in a large bowl and mix together the grains, spring onions, mint, chilli, flour and baking powder, then stir in the Filippo Berio Mild & Light Olive Oil and milk. Mix well and season to taste.

3 Heat a little Filippo Berio Mild & Light Olive Oil in a frying pan and cook 4 fritters at a time. Add heaped tablespoons of the batter, flatten with a spatula and cook for 3 minutes each side until golden and crisp. Repeat until all the batter is used up.

4 Serve with a spoonful of the aioli and a crisp salad.

Griddled Peach Salad with Cashew Cheese and Herb Dressing

This salad is rich in vitamins, antioxidants, healthy fats and irresistible Italian flavours. The herby cashew cheese is also a healthy alternative to store bought processed vegan cheese. Substitute different fruit and vegetables for whatever is in season. The cashew cheese can be stored in the fridge for up to 3 days.

Serves 2
Prep 15 mins, plus 6 hours soaking
Cook 25 mins

2	just-ripe peaches or nectarines, halved, stone removed and each cut into 8 wedges
200 g	tenderstem broccoli
1 tbsp	Filippo Berio Classico Olive Oil
250 g	cooked freekeh or quinoa
75 g	mixed watercress, spinach and rocket leaves

For the Cashew Cheese

100 g	raw cashews soaked for at least 6 hours, or overnight
	juice of ½ lemon
1	garlic clove, crushed
1 tsp	Filippo Berio White Wine Vinegar
	salt and freshly ground black pepper
2 tbsp	water
1 tbsp	freshly chopped chives

For the Herb Dressing

4 tbsp	Filippo Berio Extra Virgin Olive Oil
1 tsp	finely grated lemon zest and 2 tbsp lemon juice
1 tsp	agave nectar
4 tbsp	freshly chopped herbs, such as basil, chives and parsley

1 To make the cashew cheese, drain the soaked cashews and place in a food processor, with the lemon juice, Filippo Berio White Wine Vinegar, garlic and seasoning. Blend until you have a thick paste, scraping the sides down from time to time. Add the water 1 tbsp at a time until you have a smooth consistency. Stir in the chives. You can also make it ahead of time and refrigerate it.

2 Heat a griddle pan, when hot, add the peaches, cook for 2 minutes each side, until they have good griddle marks.

3 Meanwhile toss the broccoli in 1 tbsp of Filippo Berio Classico Olive Oil. Add to the hot griddle pan and cook for 2 minutes each side until lightly charred.

4 Whisk together all the ingredients for the dressing and season to taste.

5 Arrange the leaves on plate, scatter over the freekeh, add the broccoli and peach slices, spoon over the cheese and drizzle over the dressing.

6 Serve immediately with a good grind of black pepper.

Sweet Potato Gnocchi with Walnut and Rocket Pesto

These light potato dumplings take a little time to prepare but are worth the effort. Made simply with sweet potato, flour and a little nutmeg, we've paired the gnocchi with a nutty, peppery walnut and rocket pesto.

You can freeze the gnocchi on a tray. When frozen transfer to a freezer bag, then they can be cooked from frozen. Any left-over pesto can be stored in the fridge for up to 5 days.

Serves 3-4
Prep 10 mins
Cook 50 mins

For the Pesto

50 g	walnuts
75 g	rocket
1	garlic clove, roughly chopped
2 tbsp	nutritional yeast
125 ml	Filippo Berio Extra Virgin Olive Oil
	salt and freshly ground black pepper

For the Gnocchi

2	medium sized orange or purple sweet potatoes (about 400 g)
125 g	plain flour
	pinch grated nutmeg
	rocket leaves, to serve

1. Preheat the oven to 200°C, Gas Mark 6. Prick the potatoes all over with a fork and bake them for 40-45 minutes until tender.

2. Meanwhile make the pesto, place the rocket, walnuts, garlic and nutritional yeast in a food processor, blitz until chopped. Gradually add the Filippo Berio Extra Virgin Olive Oil, scraping down the sides of the processor, until smooth, then season well.

3. Cut the sweet potatoes in half and cool slightly, then scoop out the flesh into a bowl. Mash until smooth, stir in the nutmeg and season well. Gradually add the flour until you have a soft dough that is no longer sticky. Divide into 2 even-sized pieces, on a lightly floured surface, then roll each piece into a sausage shape about 1.5 cm wide. Then cut each into individual pieces about 2 cm long. Press down lightly on each gnocchi with the back of a fork.

4. Bring a large pan of salted water to the boil and drop in half of the gnocchi and wait for them to float to the top – this should take about 3-4 minutes. Scoop them out with a slotted spoon and place in a warm bowl. Cook the remaining gnocchi in batches.

5. Place the pesto in a large frying pan and heat gently, then stir in the gnocchi to coat. Serve immediately, with freshly ground black pepper and extra rocket leaves.

Spaghetti with Asparagus and Peas

This recipe uses some of the leftover pasta cooking water, lemon juice, garlic and chilli to create a refreshing, citrusy sauce, which pairs perfectly with the asparagus and peas. Long, thin dried pasta, such as spaghetti compliment simple olive oil-based sauces best, as they coat each pasta strand evenly without drowning it. Ideal for getting a tasty and nutritious dinner on the table in under 20 minutes!

Serves 2
Prep 5 mins
Cook 15 mins

200 g	dried spaghetti
100 g	fresh or frozen peas
2 tbsp	Filippo Berio Classico Olive Oil
150 g	asparagus tips
2	garlic cloves, thinly sliced
1	small red chilli, deseeded and thinly sliced
25 g	pine nuts
	finely grated zest and juice of 1 lemon
	salt and freshly ground black pepper
	Filippo Berio Extra Virgin Olive oil, for drizzling

1 Bring a large pan of water to the boil. Cook the pasta according to the packet instructions, adding the peas for the last 2 minutes. Drain and reserve 50 ml of the cooking water.

2 Meanwhile, heat the Filippo Berio Classico Olive Oil in a large frying pan, add the asparagus tips and cook over a gentle heat for about 3-4 minutes until they start to soften. Add the garlic and chilli and cook for a few seconds. Stir in the pine nuts and cook for 1 minute.

3 Add the drained pasta and peas to the pan and toss well. Then add the lemon zest and juice, the reserved cooking liquid, a pinch of salt and a good grind of black pepper.

4 Serve in bowls and drizzle with Filippo Berio Extra Virgin Olive Oil.

Broccoli Pesto with Penne

Originating in the beautiful coastal region of Liguria, pesto is the perfect flavoursome sauce to make at home when you're short of time – as you only need a few ingredients. For this dish, we've used a creamy broccoli and hazelnut pesto which gives it a fantastic vibrant colour. The perfect way to get your greens into a midweek meal that even the kids will eat!

Serves 2
Prep 10 mins
Cook 15 mins

200 g	wholewheat penne pasta
200 g	broccoli florets
30 g	fresh basil
1	garlic clove, crushed
25 g	roasted hazelnuts
60 ml	Filippo Berio Extra Virgin Olive Oil, plus extra for drizzling
	zest of 1 lemon
	salt and freshly ground black pepper

1 Cook the pasta in a pan of boiling water for 10 minutes, or according to packet instructions, until just tender. Drain, reserving 4 tbsp of the cooking water. Return the pasta to the warm pan.

2 Meanwhile, cook the broccoli in a pan of boiling water for 3 minutes until just tender. Drain and refresh under cold water.

3 Place the broccoli with the remaining ingredients, in a food processor, and blitz until finely chopped, adding the pasta water to loosen it. Season to taste.

4 Stir into the pasta in the pan and serve immediately in bowls, with freshly ground black pepper and a drizzle of Filippo Berio Extra Virgin Olive Oil.

Butternut Squash Risotto

The combination of butternut squash and sage is a match made in heaven and gives this risotto an autumnal twist.

Serves 4
Prep 15 mins
Cook 30 mins

3 tbsp	Filippo Berio Classico Olive Oil
1	onion, chopped
1	garlic clove, crushed
350 g	peeled butternut squash, cut into 1cm cubes
250 g	pearled spelt, rinsed
800 ml	hot vegetable stock
400 g	tinned cannellini beans, drained and rinsed
100 g	shredded cavolo nero
12	sage leaves
4 tbsp	nutritional yeast flakes
2 tbsp	vegan milk
	salt and freshly ground black pepper
	Filippo Berio Extra Virgin Olive Oil, for drizzling

1 Heat 2 tbsp of the Filippo Berio Classico Olive Oil in a saucepan, over a medium heat, cook the onion and garlic for 2-3 minutes until softened. Add the butternut squash and cook for a further 3-4 minutes, until it starts to brown.

2 Stir in the spelt and cook for 1 minute until the grains are coated in the onion mixture.

3 Pour in 100ml of the stock and cook for 2-3 minutes until absorbed. Gradually add the hot stock, 125 ml at a time, stirring constantly, until most of the liquid has been absorbed, for 15 minutes.

4 Stir in the beans and cavolo nero and cook for a further 4-5 minutes, adding the remaining stock if necessary, or until all the stock has been absorbed and the spelt is tender, but still firm.

5 Meanwhile fry the sage in the remaining oil until crisp. Stir the nutritional yeast and milk into the risotto. Serve in bowls, topped with the crispy sage leaves, freshly ground black pepper and a good drizzle of Filippo Berio Extra Virgin Olive Oil.

Caramelised Red Onion and Mushroom Pissaladiere

Just over the border of Italy, in Southern France, you'll find their take on the traditional Italian Pizza. Pissaladiere is typically made with a thicker bread dough, however for this recipe we've used ready rolled puff pastry to speed up the cooking time. Topped with sweet caramelised onions and wild mushrooms, this dish is perfect eaten hot or cold as a light snack or appetiser.

Serves 6
Prep 15 mins
Cook 50 mins

4 tbsp	Filippo Berio Classico Olive Oil
3	large red onions, thinly sliced
2 tbsp	freshly chopped thyme
1 tbsp	light muscovado sugar
2 tbsp	Filippo Berio Balsamic Vinegar
450 g	mixed wild mushrooms, sliced
2	garlic cloves, crushed
320 g	pack ready-rolled vegan puff pastry
	handful rocket leaves
	Filippo Berio Extra Virgin Olive Oil, for drizzling

1 Heat half the Filippo Berio Classico Olive Oil in a frying pan, add the onions and thyme and gently cook for 20 minutes, or until softened. Increase the heat and cook, stirring regularly, for 8 minutes or until lightly browned. Stir in the sugar and Filippo Berio Balsamic Vinegar and simmer for 5 minutes until the mixture has a jam-like consistency. Remove from the heat, season to taste and set aside.

2 Heat the remaining Filippo Berio Classico Olive Oil in a frying pan and fry the mushrooms and garlic for 5 minutes, stirring occasionally.

3 Preheat the oven, 200°C, Gas Mark 6. Unroll the pastry and place on a nonstick baking sheet. Prick the base all over with a fork.

4 Spread half the mushrooms on the base up to the edges and top with the onions, scatter over the remaining mushrooms. Bake for 20 minutes.

5 Top with the rocket and drizzle with Filippo Berio Extra Virgin Olive Oil.

Stracciatella Olive Oil Ice Cream

Originating from Northern Italy, stracciatella translates as "rags" or "shards", which is made by drizzling melted chocolate into the ice cream. The chocolate solidifies on contact with the churning ice cream turning into flakes of chocolate. For a stronger olive oil taste try making with Filippo Berio Extra Virgin Olive Oil.

Serves 6
Prep 15 mins, plus 2-3 hours chilling and freezing time

2	400ml cans coconut milk
50 g	caster sugar
2	vanilla pods, split in half lengthways
150 ml	Filippo Berio Classico Olive Oil
100 g	dark vegan chocolate
1 tbsp	Filippo Berio Classico Olive Oil

1 Place the coconut milk in a medium pan, scrape the seeds from the vanilla pods, then place the seeds and pods in the milk, with the sugar. Bring to simmering point, over a low heat, whisking until the sugar has dissolved. Bring to the boil, whisking continuously for 1 minute.

2 Remove from the heat and leave to cool slightly and infuse for 15 minutes, then remove the pods.

3 Whisk in 150 ml Filippo Berio Classico Olive Oil until well mixed.

4 Pour into a bowl, cover with cling film and chill for 2-3 hours or overnight.

5 Churn the ice cream in an ice cream machine for 20-30 minutes. Whilst the ice cream is churning, melt the chocolate and 1 tablespoon of Filippo Berio Classico Olive Oil in a small pan over a low heat. Transfer to a disposable piping bag.

6 Cut the bottom of the piping bag. Slowly drizzle most of the chocolate into the churning ice cream. Transfer to a freeze-proof container, drizzling the remaining chocolate over the top and freeze until ready to serve.

7 Remove from the freezer 5-10 minutes before serving.